Legacy Journal
MY STORY

The Moments That Made Me

Copyright © 2025 Antoinette Pellegrini

Self-published by Antoinette Pellegrini in 2025, through her business, *We Inspire Now Books*.

ISBN 978-1-7638579-3-3

This Journal is copyright. No part of this publication may be reproduced, stored in or introduced into a retrieval system, or transmitted in any form, or by any means (electronic, mechanical, photocopying, recording or otherwise) without the prior written permission of the author.

Photography: The photos in this Journal were sourced from the website: www.unsplash.com. The specific photos used in this Journal are:

a-chosen-soul-aKDa4rEJkIM-unsplash (used for the cover)
chris-tradgett-kopW25hqAkg-unsplash
felix-mittermeier-Xk0DZSYv1ao-unsplash
susan-holt-simpson-H7SCRwU1aiM-unsplash
aedrian-salazar-ECt01A5HZtw-unsplash
heather-mount-8c3zjKrkkBA-unsplash
jane-palash-KDVAiBVIO88-unsplash
chris-lawton-5IHz5WhosQE-unsplash
tolga-ahmetler-mR5Tha3uxBc-unsplash
aleksandr-gorlov-v16XSVPV1qM-unsplash
maksym-mazur-zh6hXDKbUrc-unsplash
jeremy-bishop-j06lbRyrXgw-unsplash

Design and Layout: Antoinette Pellegrini
We Inspire Now Books

We Inspire Now Books
PO BOX 133 Greensborough,
Victoria Australia 3088
www.weinspirenowbooks.com

Preface

Welcome to this *Legacy Journal*, a place for you to share the story of your life and the moments that shaped who you are. It is a story that only you can tell; a story that will be cherished by your children, grandchildren, and generations to come.

Within these pages, you'll find prompts to help you reflect on your journey and record the memories and experiences that define your life. This Journal is divided into nine chapters, with 65 thoughtful questions to guide your writing.

The first chapter invites you to begin at the beginning, with the stories you heard from your parents and grandparents. Their memories are part of your own, and by passing them on, you ensure that their voices continue to be heard.

At the end of each chapter, you'll find blank pages where you can add photographs, letters, or anything that helps bring your story to life. These pages are yours to fill in whatever way feels meaningful to you.

Take your time as you write. There is no rush and no right or wrong way to tell your story. What matters most is that it comes from your heart. Writing can be cathartic and healing, and you are encouraged to share your feelings and emotions.

This is your story, your legacy, and it deserves to be remembered.

A Snapshot

My Name: ....

Date of Birth: ....

Place of Birth: ....

My Grandparents: ....
....
....
....

Father's Name: ....

Mother's Name: ....

My Siblings: ....
....
....

My Partner: ....

My Children: ....
....

Chapter 1

Stories From My Parents and Grandparents

Who were your grandparents, and where were they born?

Where were your parents born?

If you have visited where your parents and grandparents were born, what were your impressions, and how did you feel?

When did your grandparents or parents (ancestors) come to this country, and what stories were you told about their journey?

What stories did your parents or grandparents tell you about their early lives?

Chapter 2
My Early Years

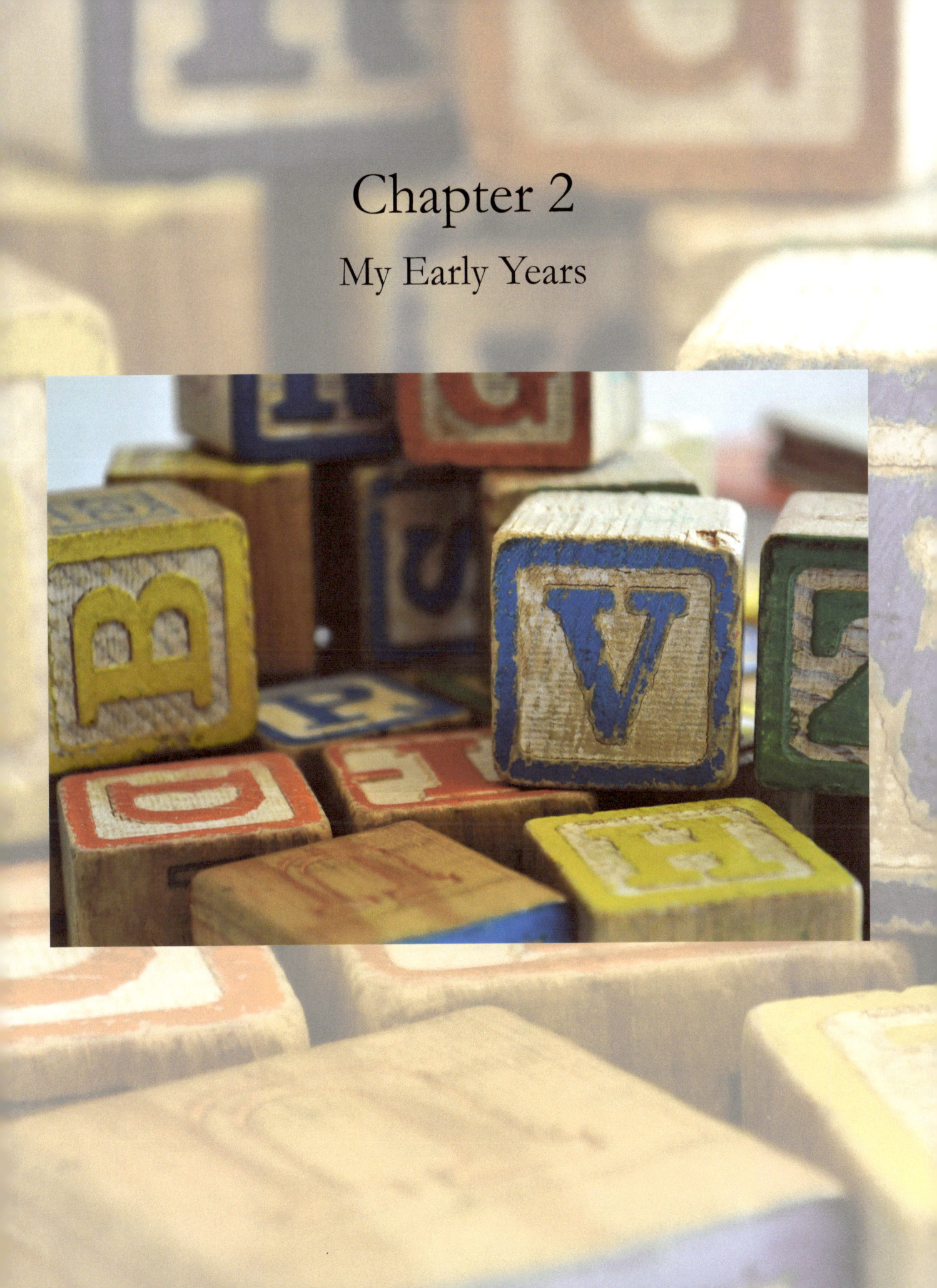

Where did you live as a child and what do you remember about the home and suburb you lived in?

What was happening in the world during your youth, and how did those events (e.g., wars, migrations, movements) affect you or your community?

What are some of your earliest memories?

Where did you go to primary school, and what are some of your memories from your primary school days?

Who were the most influential people in your early years?

Are there any other significant or funny events you can recall from early childhood?

Chapter 3
My Teenage Years

In what era were you a teenager, and what do you remember about that time?

Where did you live during your teenage years, and what were your impressions of your home and suburb at the time?

What are your most significant, happy or funny memories of your secondary school days?

Who were your friends, and what were some of the activities you did together?

Did you have a memorable teacher or classmate, and what was memorable about them?

How did schooling shape your life path?

What did you love about your teenage years?

What did you find challenging about your teenage years?

How did you get on with your parents and siblings during your teenage years, and what are some of your family memories from that time?

Did you have a job as a teenager, and if so, what was it and how did you get it?

How did you feel about turning 18, and how did you celebrate that milestone?

Is there anything else you remember, either significant or funny events that you would like to share about that time of your life?

Chapter 4
Love, Marriage and Family Life

What were you doing as a young adult in your 20s, where were you living, and were you studying, working, or in a relationship?

How did you meet your partner?

If you were married, what was your wedding like?

What experiences did you have with your partner before having children? Did you travel, and what are some significant memories from that time?

What was becoming a parent like for you, and what are the names and ages of your children?

What early memories of your children would you like to share, including any significant or funny moments?

What traditions did your family have, and what were some of the significant events and memories you shared together?

What were the highlights and challenges of your married and family life?

Are there any other significant memories of what was happening in your family life or relationships in your 30s and 40s that you would like to share?

Chapter 5

My Career and Work Life

What was your first full-time job, and how did you get it?

What other jobs did you have, and what did you love about them?

Did your career follow the path you expected, or did it change over the years?

What are the highlights, and what are you most proud of in your working life?

What challenges did you face at work?

What was it like to balance work and family?

Is there anything else you want to add about your work and career?

Chapter 6
My Beliefs and Passions
Hobbies and Travel

What activities brought you joy over the years?

Were there causes or beliefs that were important to you?

What are some of the places you've travelled that have impacted you the most, and what was significant about them, or what did you love about them?

What books, music or places influenced you most?

Is there anything else you want to share about your beliefs or passions, hobbies or travel?

Chapter 7
Growing Older

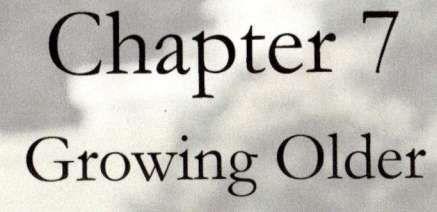

How did you feel about turning 50 and 60, and how did you celebrate those milestones?

What were the most significant events or memories of your 50s and 60s?

What changed about your job, family and relationships?

What were the highlights and challenges of this time of your life?

Is there anything else you would like to add about this time of your life?

Chapter 8
Where I Am Now

In what year are you writing this Journal? Where are you living now, and how do you feel about it?

What is most important to you in your life now?

What are you enjoying?

What are your challenges?

Do you feel you have achieved or are achieving your life goals?

Is there anything else you would like to say about your life now?

Chapter 9
My Reflections and Legacy

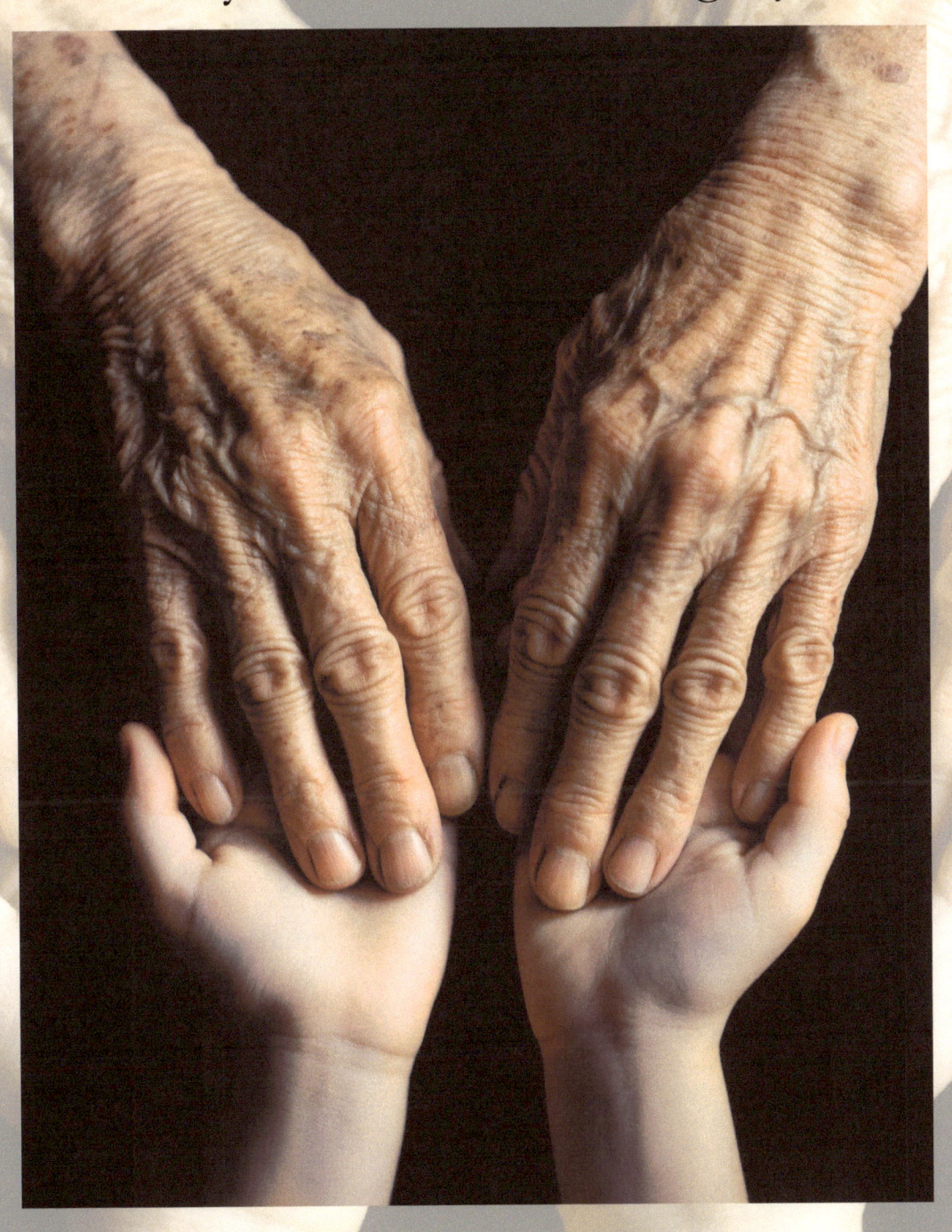

How have you seen the world change in your lifetime?

Was there a time you made a life-changing decision, and what was it?

What are the moments you now see as turning points?

What lessons have you learned from your life experiences?

If you could speak to your younger self, what would you say?

What do you want future generations to understand about your life?

What do you hope people will remember about you?

What message would you like to leave for your family?

Is there anything else you would like to add?

www.ingramcontent.com/pod-product-compliance
Lightning Source LLC
Chambersburg PA
CBHW041508220426

43661CB00017B/1279